robert
pattinson

True Love Never Dies

robert pattinson

True Love Never Dies

Josie Rusher

introduction

True Love Never Dies

Unless you've been hiding under a rock for the last year there's no way that you won't already be familiar with Robert Pattinson, star of the wildly successful movie, *Twilight*. He's been named the next Jude Law and tops lists of sexiest men on both sides of the Atlantic. This British-trained actor is heading for global success and it's no wonder why. With his smouldering good looks, eyes to lose yourself in and his trademark messed-up hair, he's the bad boy you'd run away with and the down to earth, genuine guy you'd even consider letting your parents meet. As well as his drop-dead gorgeous looks he's multi-talented. An accomplished musician who plays the piano and the guitar, this is a guy with gifts galore and the world is at his feet. Not only could he send you to heaven with his dazzling smile and endless charms, he could serenade you with a love song. Is he the perfect man? He might just be . . .

But who is the real Robert Pattinson? The guy behind the photos and the film-roles? Where has he come from to set our screens alight, and what does the future hold for him? Read on and find out all about his background, his early acting successes, what makes him tick and why he's stolen our hearts as the mysterious, immortal Edward Cullen, the sexiest vampire ever to walk the earth . . .

trivia

Name: Robert Thomas-Pattinson

Nicknames: Rob, RPattz,
Spunk Ransom, Patty

Birthdate: 13 May 1986

Starsign: Taurus

Hometown: London, England

Height: 6'1" (185cm)

Hair Colour: Brownish blond

Eye Colour: Blueish grey

Instruments: Piano and guitar

Hobbies/Sports: Football, skiing, snowboarding, pool

Favourite Actor: Jack Nicholson

Robert's celebrity crush: Kristen Stewart ('Bella' in *Twilight*)

What girl's fashion trend leaves him confused: Ugg boots

Robert's dream job: Being a professional pianist

What's his worst habit? Talking too much

Did you know? Robert was nicknamed Patty as a child because of his surname . . . it's now the name of his dog!

all about robert . . .

Family life

Robert Thomas-Pattinson was born to parents Clare and Robert Pattinson on 13 May 1986 in the London suburb of Barnes. With two sisters – Lizzy who is three years older than him and Victoria, who is five years older – Robert was the youngest of three and it's easy to see that his older sisters had a big influence on him. He's even admitted that 'up until I was 12 my sisters used to dress me up as a girl and introduce me as "Claudia"!' No wonder he's used to role playing!

And Robert can learn a lot about life as a star from his sisters too. Lizzy is an established singer and the songwriting brains behind lots of catchy chart hits. When she was just 17 she was spotted by EMI whilst singing in her local pub in Barnes and within a year she had gone from being the star singer in her high school concert to a top ten bestselling artist in the UK with the band Aurora. Dealing with this sudden rise to fame must have been challenging as, like Robert,

'up until I was 12 my sisters used to dress me up as a girl and introduce me as "Claudia"!'

'When I was flying to Rome, we flew over London; I felt like bursting into tears. It's part of me, so I can't leave London behind for good.'

Lizzy was keen to continue at school so that she'd always have something to fall back on, showing a level-headed ambition that runs in the family. Since then Lizzy has been living a jet set lifestyle, touring major venues in the UK, North America and Europe to perform in front of thousands of screaming fans. Victoria, Robert's eldest sister, decided to steer clear of the cameras and microphones and works instead on the other side of the media in advertising. But it's not just his sisters that influenced him. Robert inherited his classic good looks from his mum, Clare, who worked in the modelling industry when Robert was growing up and Robert's dad, Richard, also recently revealed that he had a creative side. Richard has always been the classic businessman, importing and selling vintage cars, so Robert had never thought of him as particularly artistic: 'I was shocked as I never saw him as a creative. I think me and my sisters are living out that side of him.' It really is in his genes!

School days

Robert Pattinson grew up in the affluent, leafy area of Barnes, just down river from the buzzing capital, London. As one of the entertainment centres of the world, what better place for any aspiring movie star to grow up? Robert's first school, Tower House School, an all-boys school in Barnes, nurtured this creativity and encouraged all its pupils to pursue their creative ambitions from a young age. At just six years old, Robert was already shining on stage, starring in numerous school productions including *Spell for a Rhyme* and William Golding's cult classic, *The Lord of the Flies*. He clearly had star calibre from the outset but unlike model-student, Cedric Diggory, who Robert would go on to play in the Harry Potter movies, Robert was far more interested in acting and drama than being top of the class. In a 1998 school newsletter he was described as the 'runaway winner of last term's Form Three untidy desk award'! But gorgeous Robert was making an impression on his friends and teachers in other ways too. In an interview with the *Evening Standard*, the school secretary revealed that Robert 'was an absolutely lovely boy, everyone adored him. We have lots of lovely boys here but he was something special. He was very pretty, beautiful and blond.'

According to Robert, a turning point came when he was 12 and moved to the Harrodian School, a mixed, private school in southwest London. As a naturally creative person it's no wonder that school was a bit of a mixed bag for Robert – it offered an outlet for his creativity but with the new distraction of girls and the discovery of hair gel, he also found it difficult to find a focus. Robert confesses that 'school reports were always pretty bad – I never ever did

my homework. I always turned up for lessons as I liked my teachers but my report said I didn't try very hard.' This is the first glimpse of that formidable mix that makes Robert so appealing: the mischievous bad-boy coupled with charm and a heart of gold. By the time he was 12, Robert's rebellious streak had got him in trouble and he was expelled from school. But this was just the wake up call that Robert needed and with a fair amount of persuasion from his dad, Robert decided to join the local acting school, Barnes Theatre Group. The fact that the Theatre Group also attracted lots of pretty girls must have made it seem even more appealing! At this stage, the young Robert

'12 was a turning point as I moved to a mixed school and then I became cool and discovered hair gel.'

thought the drama school thing was just a great way to have fun and meet girls. Rather than acting straight off, Robert began by helping out backstage. Even now that he is heralded as one of the hottest acting talents on the planet, he still says 'I haven't really decided to be an actor yet!' and in true Robert style, he says he just kind of fell into the profession. It's difficult to imagine that a guy with so much talent would be shy, but Robert confesses to being less confident when he was growing up and he never really considered pushing himself out onto centre stage in any serious way. Luckily for us, one day Robert just thought he'd try out for a chorus part in a production of *Guys and Dolls*. It was a small bit part as a Cuban dancer but when he got the part, his star potential was obvious and in the next production, Robert took the lead role.

Robert says 'it is unbelievable how this stroke of luck has completely changed my entire life ... I owe everything to that little club.' Given that so many celebrities forget their roots and the people that helped them get where they are, it's refreshing to see that Robert, despite his hectic international schedule, still takes time to remember how he got to where he is. This is just typical of Robert's down-to-earth personality.

By the time he had stepped into the front ranks at Barnes Theatre Group, Robert had already been scouted for his stunning looks – *that* hair and *those* eyes – and had been modelling since he was 12. So it was only a matter of time before the combination of his acting skills and his looks caught the attention of the showbiz world. He was officially spotted in a production of *Tess of the D'Urbervilles* and after that he started looking for professional roles. Robert soon started creeping his way up the 'ones to watch' lists of some of London's biggest TV and theatre casting directors and before long he was appearing in the television film *Ring of the Nibelungs* and the DVD version of Mira Nair's *Vanity Fair*. It was the earnings from *Ring of the Nibelungs* that paid for his final two years worth of fees at the Harrodian School. Robert's dad suggested that Robert leave school at 16 but, still unsure what he wanted to do with his life, Robert said he'd pay for his own fees. The agreement was that if Robert got good enough grades, his dad would repay the fees. So did he get the grades?! Nope!

It was at this point that Robert's wild-boy image got another moment to show itself. Despite being slated to star in the stage production of *The Woman Before* in May 2005, he was fired shortly before the opening night. But by this point, legendary director Mike Newell had already heard the buzz around Robert and was intent on getting him involved in the Harry Potter movies . . .

harry potter

'I've changed so much. I'm not nearly as cocky as I was.'

Before getting his big break with his role as Cedric Diggory in *Harry Potter and the Goblet of Fire*, Robert had already enjoyed a small taste of the celebrity his career would bring him. Nothing could prepare him, however, for the mega success of the films, nor the Pottermania which accompany them. Robert explained the big change to his life as happening literally overnight: 'The day before [the film was released] I was just sitting in Leicester Square, happily being ignored by everyone. Then suddenly strangers are screaming your name. Amazing.' Describing the film as a 'huge step and a massive event in my life', it's not surprising that being catapulted into the limelight and onto the red carpet would affect him. Looking back on that initial craziness, Robert admits that it took him a while to adjust: 'I've changed so much. I'm not nearly as cocky as I was. I was a real prat for the first month. I didn't talk to anyone.' It shows what an honest, nice guy Robert is that he can admit to getting a little full of himself. And the fact that he made sure that the cockiness didn't last says a lot about

Robert on Daniel Radcliffe (Harry Potter):

'I think Daniel's . . . just so far superior to me in terms of desirability, so he didn't really have much of a competition with me. If was I was Katie, I would definitely go out with him because he's rich and famous, and I'm not really!'

the strength of his character. Dealing with such a massive success so suddenly would be a shock for anyone. But the experience of working on a mega-blockbuster film series where books with cult popularity were to be transformed into big-budget Hollywood films with equally big cult popularity was to stand him in good stead for his future role as Edward Cullen in *Twilight*. Robert hadn't read the books within the Harry Potter series before getting the part but as soon as he found out he immersed himself in its universe, reading *Harry Potter and the Goblet of Fire* 'loads and loads of times' as the shoots took place. But he didn't just stop at reading the books – he also raided the huge number of Harry Potter websites and fan forums out on the internet, picking up tips from the fans and getting to grips with how the fans saw his character. It's this dedication and passion for his work which lends Robert his magical on-screen charm and the ability to convincingly flesh out the characters he portrays.

Joining the crew

But how was Robert to take to the challenge of joining the cast and crew of Harry Potter and what did he make of the role itself? If you're a fan of the books you'll know that Cedric Diggory is a role that Robert was born for – the fair-playing, sporty, impossibly good-looking prefect who wins Harry's respect by his displays of sportsmanship. Although pitched against each other in Quidditch and in the Triwizard Tournament, Cedric and Harry form a bond which grows ever closer. Initially fighting against each other, they soon turn to fight alongside each other as they unite against the evil Lord Voldemort, right up

until the tragic turn where Cedric is murdered by He Who Must Not be Named.

Robert's chiselled cheekbones and cut-glass accent made him perfect for the role, and it was one that he relished playing, enjoying the chance to play an old-fashioned hero. Talking about the part, Robert describes Cedric as a 'pretty cool character. He's not really a complete cliché of the good kid in school. He's just quiet. He is actually just a genuine person.' Playing a genuine good guy might have been straight-forward, but it was having to fill the script's demands for an 'absurdly handsome 17-year-old' that freaked Robert out! With some modelling experience already under his belt, he rose to the challenge admirably. But for modest Robert the task of 'trying to get good angles to look good-looking' was 'much scarier than meeting Voldemort!' And going into such a big production must have been daunting in itself. Although he'd worked with a small special effects crew in *Ring of the Nibelungs*, working with some 2000 people on the set of Harry Potter came as a very different experience. Trying to stay composed whilst rushing around the maze scene during the Third Task of the Triwizard Tournament was a challenge that Robert described as 'enforced method acting' – there was no need to fake the excitement and tension! As he put it himself, 'We were really hyped up. You are on 100% adrenaline and you're starting this in the first week and you have just met all the other actors the week before and now you have to go crazy with them. That was pretty intense, but I think it was really the most fun, because it was really physical work.' The physical side of it was a new thing for Robert, and as he had to play the role of Hogwart's super-fit Cedric there was some preparation to do for the role alongside learning

Robert on
Katie Leung
(Cho Chang):

'I get on really well with Katie, she's a really cool girl.'

the lines! It must have come as a bit of a shock when Robert tried out the costume for the swimming scene – a pair of skimpy trunks – and was picked up on his physique by the costume designer, who said 'Aren't you supposed to be fit? You could be playing a sissy poet or something!' Ouch. Not having taken much in the way of exercise for about six months, maybe this didn't come as too much of a surprise to Robert. But the phone call the next day must have. He was called up by the assistant director who told him they'd be putting him on a personal training programme. 'I thought that would be pretty cool,' says Robert, 'because it would make me take it seriously.' By his own admission, when he started the course he couldn't even manage ten press-ups, but after a while it started to pay off. At the start, however, he admits that co-star Daniel Radcliffe's chest was about twice the size of his own!

Speaking about his co-stars it's clear that Robert became very close to them during the making of the film. Going straight into a team of people who were used to working with each other, including some of Britain's finest actors such as Michael Gambon and Ralph Fiennes as well as the younger cast, who've become superstars in their own right, was initially a big leap, and Robert admits to getting a bit star-struck by the three main stars – Daniel Radcliffe, Emma Watson and Rupert Grint – when he first met them. 'I couldn't get it out of my head that like "you're Harry Potter!" but . . . everyone was friendly. It's a very relaxed set.' Fortunately, the beginning of the shoot saw the actors doing a lot of improvisation together which helped them to bond. And it must have helped that he was working with such a talented, funny, intelligent group of people.

Robert on Ralph Fiennes (Lord Voldemort): 'I was quite intimidated by Ralph Fiennes. I didn't really talk to him while I was doing Harry Potter and the only thing I did with him was when he stepped on my head. Then I went to this play and he was there. And this girl said, "you've worked with Ralph Fiennes haven't you, Robert?" and I was like, "well, no . . . " and Ralph said, "yes, I stepped on your head." And that was the extent of our conversation.'

Moving on . . .

Robert returned to the big screen in a flashback episode in *Harry Potter and the Order of the Phoenix* but by now his sights were set further afield. As a consequence of his brilliant performance in Harry Potter he'd been named a 'British Star of Tomorrow' by *Times Online*. Suddenly doors were beginning to open . . . Still, the exhaustion involved in working on such a well-oiled, movie-juggernaut as Harry

Potter must have taken its toll, as Robert took some time off to hang out in Los Angeles before returning to London. He's described his choice to take it easy for a short while as having 'squandered away' the momentum of his Harry Potter appearances but it certainly did him no harm. Returning to London, to live with his best friend in a tiny apartment with just one chair, a TV and homemade furniture, must have been a weird jolt back to the land of the living. But he remembers this period fondly, even nostalgically: 'It was so cool . . . you had to walk through a restaurant kitchen to get up to the roofs but you could, like, walk along all the roofs . . . I didn't do anything for a year, I just sat on the roof and played music . . . it was like the best time I had ever had.' The fact that Robert kept his feet firmly on the ground and didn't get swept up in a tide of Hollywood excess or start taking himself too seriously just goes to show what a real, genuine person he is. He may well be the best-looking guy on the planet but he's not just a pretty face – he's a grounded guy with real depth of character.

Devoting himself to his music wasn't a new thing for Robert, as he'd been playing music well before he set his sights on acting. Nonetheless, wheels were now in motion: he'd been given his big break, the hard work had paid off, and it was time to take the limelight properly and step into the acting role of a lifetime . . .

'I didn't do anything for a year, I just sat on the roof and played music.'

twilight

True Love Never Dies

I f playing the role of a perfect prefect was challenging
enough to live up to, it would be as nothing compared
to Robert's next role. He would have to be nothing less than
the perfect man, the hero at the heart of Stephenie Meyer's
epic *Twilight* saga. It's hard to overstate just how much
expectation Robert was about to take on his shoulders by
taking on the role of Edward Cullen, the brooding, complex,
eternally beautiful young man at the heart of the hit book
series. This time Robert wouldn't just be stepping into a
supporting role alongside the film's lead, he'd actually be
the lead actor himself.

Twilight started out as a dream in the mind of Stephenie
Meyer, the American author who's been billed as the next
J.K. Rowling. She dreamt of a normal human girl and
a beautiful vampire who was in love with her but who
thirsted after her blood. And it's from this tiny acorn that
the mighty oak of the *Twilight* saga developed. Her series
of four books has sold over 25 million copies worldwide
– an astonishing number – and have earned her millions

of devoted fans and well over a hundred fan sites on the web. The series follows the story of Isabella 'Bella' Swan, a teenager who moves miles across the country to live with her father, leaving a world of Arizonan sunshine and heat for the damp and miserable Forks, Washington. On starting at her new school Bella meets Edward Cullen, played by Robert, and is drawn in by his enigmatic, mysterious, handsome charm. Little does she know that Edward is part of a family of vampires – blessed with eternal youth but damned by a constant craving for blood. Bella can't

Stephenie Meyer on Robert's performance:
'It's really too bad in some ways because *Twilight* is going to be limited by the fact that this is a vampire romance and it's basically aimed at teens. If not for that, his performance in my opinion is Oscar-worthy.'

understand why Edward behaves coldly towards her, unaware that he is so attracted to Bella's scent that he has to use all his willpower just to stop himself from taking her and drinking her blood. Yet the magnetism between them is so incredibly powerful that Bella and Edward are drawn together, and it soon becomes clear that they are destined to be with one another. Many have compared the saga to the story of Shakespeare's *Romeo and Juliet* and there's definitely more than a passing resemblance to that great tale of two star-crossed lovers. As Robert describes it, it's a 'very deep love story'. But the genius of Meyer's imagination was to combine a heart-melting story of true love with the passion and thrills of a gothic horror novel.

It's no surprise that the hugely popular book series should have caught the attention of Hollywood's gaze, and it was almost inevitable that a blockbuster film should follow in its wake. In *Twilight* the movie, released in the US on 21 November 2008 and in the UK on 19 December, the director Catherine Hardwicke has turned the author's dream and the fantasy of the book into the flesh and blood of a film, with an array of talented, hot young actors. And who better than Robert to be at the very heart of them?

'Every woman has their
own Edward.'

– Rachelle Lefevre

Fulfilling the fan's fantasy

But there's no way Robert was going to just walk into the part. He was still virtually unknown as an actor outside of the Harry Potter films, and for a film this big there was always going to be huge competition for the leading role. In fact, Stephenie Meyer's first choice for the role was an actor named Henry Cavill. But by the time it came round to the film being produced Cavill was 25 and it would have been difficult for him to play the role of a youthful 17-year-old – especially with the possibility of three movie

sequels in mind. Still, some 5000 other hopefuls were to put themselves forward for the role of Edward so the coast was by no means clear. With Cavill out of the running, Robert made it to the shortlist. The other most popular fan suggestions for actors to play Edward were Hayden Christensen (most famous for playing the young Anakin Skywalker in *Star Wars*), Orlando Bloom and Gerard Way (singer with the band My Chemical Romance). Having seen a picture of Robert from his role in Harry Potter, Hardwicke was unconvinced that he was the right guy for the role. So Robert flew out to Venice to meet Hardwicke and convince her in person. To do so, he had to audition a love scene with Kristen Stewart, the beautiful actress who had already been picked to play Edward's lover, Bella. Robert's smouldering yet restrained passion and his instant rapport with Kristen set the room on fire, and in that moment it was obvious that Robert's ethereal beauty and charm made him the perfect Edward Cullen.

Of course, the rest is history, but Robert admits with characteristic modesty that he never expected to get the break, largely because the role needed someone who was so beautiful that it would hurt to look at them, someone who was just incredibly stunning. 'That's kind of why I was kind of tortured before the casting. I read the book and was like "Well this is really dumb. It's just so pointless, even going up for it."' Modest Robert obviously didn't see what the rest of the casting crew were able to witness. But even with the part in the bag

Robert on being asked how he approached the kissing scenes in the movie:

'I kinda just approached it from the front . . .'

the battle still wasn't over. With legions of fans worldwide eagerly anticipating the film adaptation, everyone had their own favourite choice for the role, and Robert wasn't one of them! Fans were bewildered when the role went to a Brit actor who they'd not even heard of. A furore erupted on fansites worldwide and it was only when Stephenie Meyer herself stepped in to defend Robert that things calmed down! Speaking about it later, she explained that 'the way he took it was a lot more positive than the way I would have handled it. He was like "I'm going to prove them wrong. I'm going to go out there and prove them wrong." The movie hasn't come out yet and he's won over 99.9% of the people who didn't approve of him as Edward. And when they see the movie, oh my gosh, there's no way not to love him!' Now, months later, with the film out, it's likely that 99.9% is going to become a straight 100% ...

Acting the part ...

So the balls were rolling. But transforming himself into the role of a 108-year-old vampire with superpowers and an unquenchable lust for blood wasn't going to just happen without some serious hard work. Robert hadn't even had a chance to read the books before the casting session so it was now time to delve deep into the world of the *Twilight* saga and really get to grips with the complex character he was about to play. Describing the role, Robert calls Edward a 'conflicted and reluctant vampire. He's a poet, and very deep and profound. He's just extraordinarily troubled.' Fortunately, Robert's own intensely creative personality lent itself perfectly to the role, and fellow vampire Kellan Lutz, who plays Edward's onscreen brother, Emmett Cullen, wasn't the only one to point out the similarities between actor and role: 'Rob is definitely Edward. He's so complicated, so poetic . . .' The tragic side of Edward was something that Robert wanted to bring out in the role, seeing it as key to making his character convincing. And it's also an element that's at the heart of the tortured love story between Edward and Bella: how can he, an immortal vampire, live with a normal, mortal girl, and how can he reconcile his desire to devour her with his desire to care for her and his all-consuming love for her? To do this he has to battle against his base instincts, and it's only through Bella's belief in him – by telling him 'I'm not scared of you. You're not a monster' – that Edward finds the strength to believe in himself. Being such a sensitive guy, Robert had all the tools within himself to really place himself inside the complicated character of Edward. But he took it further, just going to show, once again, his passion and

'Rob is definitely Edward. He's so complicated, so poetic...'

dedication to his craft. In order to prepare for the role he began writing journal entries as Edward and also took the brave and difficult step to distance himself from his friends and family so that he could 'feel his isolation' and understand what it must be like to actually *be* Edward – to be separated from the world around him in the way that only an immortal vampire could be. 'I was thinking that he's just a normal guy who got bitten by someone,' says Robert; 'I guess I just tried to think, if you've been bitten by some guy when you're unconscious and you wake up and you're eternal and you have super-strength and super-speed and you want to kill people and drink their blood and before that you're a perfectly normal 17-year-old . . . '

There was also the physical side of the role to consider. Not seeing himself as an 'action movie kind of guy at all', this didn't come so easily to him as getting inside the role of Edward. However, it didn't stop him from impressing his

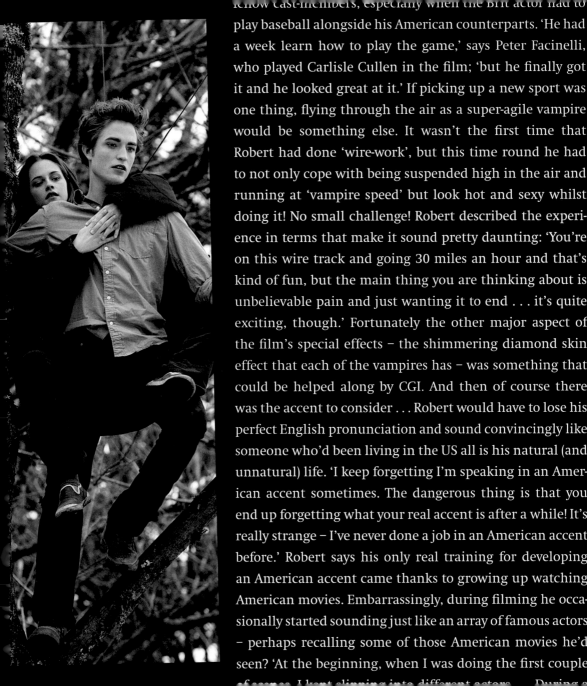

know cast-members, especially when the Brit actor had to play baseball alongside his American counterparts. 'He had a week learn how to play the game,' says Peter Facinelli, who played Carlisle Cullen in the film; 'but he finally got it and he looked great at it.' If picking up a new sport was one thing, flying through the air as a super-agile vampire would be something else. It wasn't the first time that Robert had done 'wire-work', but this time round he had to not only cope with being suspended high in the air and running at 'vampire speed' but look hot and sexy whilst doing it! No small challenge! Robert described the experience in terms that make it sound pretty daunting: 'You're on this wire track and going 30 miles an hour and that's kind of fun, but the main thing you are thinking about is unbelievable pain and just wanting it to end . . . it's quite exciting, though.' Fortunately the other major aspect of the film's special effects – the shimmering diamond skin effect that each of the vampires has – was something that could be helped along by CGI. And then of course there was the accent to consider . . . Robert would have to lose his perfect English pronunciation and sound convincingly like someone who'd been living in the US all is his natural (and unnatural) life. 'I keep forgetting I'm speaking in an American accent sometimes. The dangerous thing is that you end up forgetting what your real accent is after a while! It's really strange – I've never done a job in an American accent before.' Robert says his only real training for developing an American accent came thanks to growing up watching American movies. Embarrassingly, during filming he occasionally started sounding just like an array of famous actors – perhaps recalling some of those American movies he'd seen? 'At the beginning, when I was doing the first couple

really dramatic scene, you start doing Al Pacino!' Robert's described another Hollywood great, Jack Nicholson, as one of his early teen idols – someone he aspired to be like and whose accent he copied. But who knows, it's probably a matter of time before other young aspiring actors are copying Robert's accent and style!

No-one can now be in any doubt that Robert rose to the role as no other actor could have done and has acquitted himself brilliantly. Fans of the books now accept Robert as the perfect incarnation of Edward and have been going crazy for him since the film was first shown. At the film's premiere in Los Angeles there were 25 bodyguards on standby to protect him from the huge crowds of hysterical fans. 'Everyone just screams and screams and screams. I have accepted it as real now, but it still feels surreal.' At heart Robert is still the boy from Barnes, but he's managed to also become the embodiment of millions of fans' dreams – Edward Cullen, perhaps the greatest romantic hero ever to be conjured up by a writer's imagination . . .

Bella & Edward

Kristen on Robert:

'I think he's really handsome.'

Bella Swan, the beautiful 17-year-old who is at the centre of the story and from whose perspective the books in the *Twilight saga* are written, started out in Stephenie Meyer's imagination as just 'an average girl' – someone any young woman could relate to. As time went on and the character developed in Meyer's mind, she decided upon the name 'Isabella'. In her words, 'after spending so much time with the character, I loved her like a daughter . . . Inspired by that love, I gave her the name I was saving for my daughter . . . Isabella.'

Fortunately for Meyer and director Catherine Hardwicke they found the perfect casting in Kristen Stewart, a relatively experienced actress who'd come fresh from starring in Sean Penn's critically acclaimed film *Into the Wild*. Stewart seemed able to capture the wise-beyond-her-years quality of Bella as well as her unfussy, down to earth nature. And it's obvious for all to see that the onscreen chemistry between Robert and Kristen was there right from the start. After visiting the set, Meyer said the chemistry was so strong and so powerful that it 'may cause hyperventilation'. So it's no surprise that fans who've watched the film have been left breathless!

Robert on Kristen:

'Kristen's the best actress of our generation.'

music and
romance

'Music is my backup plan
if acting fails.'

Anyone who knows Robert knows one key fact about him:
he's an all-round creative type who isn't just gifted at
acting – he's also a hugely talented singer-songwriter. He's
able to play the piano like a virtuoso and sings along to his
own compositions on the guitar.

He recently revealed that when he was 14 he fronted a
rap trio that was 'pretty hard-core for three private school
kids from suburban London.' Although from what he says,
perhaps it wasn't as hard-core as all that? He added, 'And
my mum's, like, cramping our style, popping her head in to
ask, "You boys want a sandwich?"' In fact, Robert has redis-
covered his love for rap and explained 'I've really gotten
into hip-hop again recently. I'm reliving my childhood. I've
been listening to a lot of Wu-Tang Clan. I always wanted
to be a rapper when I was younger. That's always what I
wanted to be before I started acting.' But he's the first to
admit that he might not be the most obvious candidate for
living up to the image of a gun-toting gangster rap-artist:

'Music is kind of a
big part of my life . . .
I go through phases,
especially when I'm in
London, where all I
do is play music.'

'I didn't have the right physicality about it – I'm not very threatening!' When Robert is in London he sings in a band called Bad Girls and has also developed himself as a solo artist, performing under the stage name of Bobby Dupea. But his passion for music started a long time ago, as Robert explains: 'I have been playing the piano for my entire life – since I was three or four. And the guitar – I used to play classical guitar from when I was about five to 12 years of age. Then I didn't play guitar for like years. About four or five years ago, I got out the guitar again and just started playing blues and stuff.' That blues element has become part of his sound, so it's no wonder that there's more than a touch of Led Zeppelin's bluesy rock sound to be found in the songs Robert has co-written with Bad Girls.

In the past, his two worlds of music and acting have been separate as he's focused on each one in turn, but with *Twilight* he was given the amazing opportunity to bring the two together. He has written and performed two earthy, spine-tingling ballads, 'Never Think', which appears on the official movie soundtrack, and 'Let Me

Sign'. 'Never Think' is a beautiful, soulful song, full of emotion, and if you thought Robert couldn't get much sexier, you should see him singing this! But apparently their inclusion in the film was purely accidental. An anonymous third party had given star director Catherine Hardwicke the disk without Robert knowing! The self-effacing actor can't quite get used to it: 'When I went to see the cut [of the film] she'd put these two songs in. They're old songs, but one of them specifically, it really made the scene better . . . I'm singing it, maybe that makes it different, but it's kind of overwhelming. I *hope* it's overwhelming.' And director Hardwicke certainly thinks so: 'One of my favourite parts of making the movie was watching Rob play the music he wrote. He just lets it out, and it breaks your heart.'

On his style, Robert is modest about what it takes to be a matinee idol. Asked how he gets his hair looking so ruffled and sexy he put it down to wearing a hat a lot! 'I have so much residue crap in my hair from years and years of not washing it and not having any sense of personal hygiene whatsoever . . . even today, I go into these things where I'm supposed to be this sexy guy or whatever, and I'm literally asking, "if I get plumes of dandruff on me, can you just brush it off?"' He swears by not washing his hair, following the age-old maxim that if you leave it unwashed for long enough it starts washing itself . . . Hmmm. But then, who is complaining when he looks this good?!

It's his natural unfussy, down-to-earth attitude that is really appealing. Well that and his amazingly sexy eyes! He's not artificial or vain – he is who he is and doesn't try too hard at it. Despite his stunning good looks, Robert seems unable to see it himself. When asked whether he thought he was a 'sexy man-beast' he answered, 'I wouldn't be able to say. I don't think I'm much of one. It's funny, it is the secret to any guy – if people find him unattractive or whatever you just get Stephenie Meyer to tell the world, to put on her Web site that this guy is now attractive and everybody changes their minds.' It's this self-deprecating charm that makes him all the more attractive.

So we all know what's fascinating about Robert, but what does *he* look for in a girl? 'I'm always shocked by the people who I'm attracted to. It's always completely random. I generally like people who are a bit crazy but yeah, that's pretty much my only prerequisite.' The first love of Robert's life lasted for ten years. But amazingly he never properly spoke to her. He explains 'when I finally told her she was like, "You've never spoken to me in my whole life. You've only spoken to me about three times and never said anything nice,"' but for Robert 'that's the best type of love'. It's true that love that lives in the imagination, without restraint, can live forever. All that it needs to survive is hope. Perhaps this experience of unrequited love and romance gave him valuable experience to draw on when acting out the forbidden, dangerous love between Edward and Bella?

Robert is rumoured to have dated Annelyse Schoenberger, the gorgeous Brazilian model, as well as sultry actress Nikki Read, but it looks as though sexy Robert is yet to be tied down. There have been tons of rumours about Robert and his beautiful co-star Kristen Stewart and, aside from their obvious respect for each other's acting credentials, there is certainly a lot of chemistry between the gorgeous pair. It could be the hottest celebrity pairing in Hollywood! Robert has admitted that Kristen is his biggest celebrity crush but is yet to confirm that there is anything more than mutual admiration between them. Watch this space . . .

'I'm always shocked by the people who I'm attracted to.'

51

Interviewer: 'What would you say to parents who thought you were bad news for their daughter?'

Robert: 'You're right . . . '

53

beyond twilight

True Love Never Dies

You might think that now Robert has landed the role of a lifetime and become a global star life would be easy sailing from here on in. For an actor who was simply after fame and success then maybe that would be right, but for Robert – the cultured, sensitive, incredibly talented guy that can act, sing and bowl you over with his smile – the options are endless. He's always stayed true to his roots and has no desire to be famous just for the sake of celebrity, unlike so many others. So why is he different? On being asked if he wants to be a megastar, Robert simply put it like this: 'No, I can't see any advantage to it, because I'm happy with the life I nave now . . . I've got the same two friends I've had since I was 12, and I can't see that changing.' He hasn't bought into the whole Hollywood glitz and hasn't changed his style since becoming a star. Just as well, as in typically down to earth style he hates shopping for clothes! He hasn't got a car – or a girlfriend – and he lives with a friend in a rented flat in Soho, London. He keeps it real by

making sure his feet stay firmly on the ground. He's openly spoken about how, in the past, he became disillusioned with the whole experience of acting and very nearly gave the whole thing up. He explained that this was 'mainly because most movies being made now are designed in such a way that it's all about making a lot of money . . . I'm not interested in simply adding more s*** to the pile. I'd rather just not be a part of it, in that case.' Thank god he had a change of heart and realised that he could be involved with film-work that wasn't just about the money and which had real artistic value to it. Still, he won't put all his eggs in one basket and has described music as his back-up plan if the acting fails. Fortunately for us, it looks as though Robert will be lighting up our screens for a long time to come and with a bit of luck he'll continue to wow us with his beautiful song-writing too . . .

'Sometimes I think,
"to hell with acting," and then
I realize I could be working at a shoe shop.
Acting is much cooler.'

How to Be

Alongside *Twilight*, Robert has been working on a number of other film projects slated for release in the near future. In all of them Robert brings his excellent acting skills to bear on varied roles. In *How to Be*, written and directed by Oliver Irving, Robert plays the role of Art, a young man with aspirations as a singer-songwriter, struggling to find balance in his life. Sound familiar?! Robert's astounding performance won him the 'Best Actor in a Feature' award at the Strasbourg Film Festival in September 2008 and has gone on to make the official selection at leading film festivals around the world. If there are parallels to be drawn between Robert's own life experiences and those of Edward Cullen, there are also connections with Art, as Robert brings out a heart-breaking vulnerability to both roles, showing his depth as an actor. He immediately caught the attention of director Oliver Irving when he began improvising during his casting session, which was, according to Irving, 'exactly what I wanted – someone who could just become the character and leave behind the kind of "techniques" trained in at drama schools. I had a hunch he would work well with other cast and would be able to get across the kind of naivety inherent to Art's character. He's a really down to earth guy . . . ' True to his style and modest as ever, Robert downplayed the fact that he'd appeared in the Harry Potter films when he was at the casting, and it wasn't until later on that Oliver Irving watched *Harry Potter and the Goblet of Fire* and realised that Robert had been one of the major roles. And likewise, when he was asked about his musical abilities he simply said he could only muster a few chords!

It looks as though the massive success of *Twilight* will fan the flames of success for *How to Be*, as the more attention Robert gets for his role as Edward Cullen the more interest there'll be in his smaller projects, whether that's films or music.

Little Ashes

Another film in which Robert is set to shine is *Little Ashes,* written by Philippa Goslett and directed by Paul Morrison, which explores the complex relationship between the young Surrealist painter Salvador Dali and the poet Federico García Lorca. Robert plays none other than the creative genius himself, Dali, showing him at the threshold of his career as a painter. Unsurprisingly, Robert brings his trademark blend of smouldering sex appeal and sensitivity to convey the young Dali as a conflicted, shy and confused young man. The film was actually shot before *Twilight*, although it's scheduled for release in 2009. Speaking about the film, Robert explained that working on it offered a fantastic training ground for his subsequent preparation work on *Twilight*: 'It was the first job I had where I had an opportunity to really obsess over something, and I brought that mentality into *Twilight*, doing that as well.'

The saga continues . . .

Fans of Stephanie Meyer's *Twilight* saga will be nursing a vampiric hunger for the next instalments in the series, and thankfully for us, Robert has already confirmed that he's signed up for the next two sequels to *Twilight*: *New Moon* and *Eclipse*. But what's next? And what does the future hold beyond the twilight?

It's clear that Robert's ambitious and broad-minded nature leaves lots of options open for him. He's even hinted at an interest in producing and directing films in the future, having expressed huge admiration for Mike Newell, who directed him in *Harry Potter*. And it's also clear that he's keen to expand his range of film-acting through working with other directors, referencing the likes of Jean-Luc Godard, Michael Cimino and Terry Gilliam as people he'd love to work with. And with Robert's natural abilities directors will undoubtedly be queuing up to work with him too. As Catherine Hardwicke explained, reflecting on his brilliant turn as Edward, 'his career could be extremely unique . . . He's a powerful, sexy leading man and slips incredibly well into different periods and styles. I'd also love to see him work on Tim Burton-esque films where he has the opportunity to create completely wild, original characters that become classics.'

One things for certain, with Robert's natural assets we're set to see a whole lot more of him over the coming years. Although he will shine in other roles, in our hearts, our dreams and our imagination, Robert Pattinson will forever live on as the beautiful, enigmatic Edward Cullen . . .

'He's a powerful, sexy leading man and slips incredibly well into different periods and styles.'

62

Picture credits

Rex: 8, 9, 10, 18, 26, 30, 31, 32, 38, 40, 41 (bottom), 42, 45
Getty: 2, 4, 6, 12, 20, 25, 28, 34-35, 36, 37, 39, 41 (top), 44, 46, 49, 52-3, 54, 59, 61, 63
PA: 7, 13, 14, 17, 48, 56-7, 58 (bottom)
Big Pictures: 15, 23, 43, 50, 51
Corbis: 21, 58 (top)
iStock: Inside covers

Acknowledgements

Josie Rusher would like to thank Daniel Bunyard, Jane Sturrock and Helen Ewing,
without whom this book wouldn't have been possible, and all the other wonderful
people who helped make this book a reality including Malcolm Edwards,
Mark Rusher, Rich Carr, Kate Oliver, Fiona McIntosh and Charlie Panayiotou.

First published in hardback in Great Britain in 2008 by
Orion Books
an imprint of the Orion Publishing Group Ltd
Orion House, 5 Upper St Martin's Lane,
London WC2H 9EA
An Hachette UK Company

1 3 5 7 9 10 8 6 4 2

A CIP catalogue record for this book is available
from the British Library.

ISBN: 978-1-4091-1263-1

Design: www.carrstudio.co.uk
Printed in Spain by Cayfosa

The Orion Publishing Group's policy is to use papers that are natural, renewable and
recyclable and made from wood grown in sustainable forests. The logging and manufacturing
processes are expected to conform to the environmental regulations of the country of origin.

Every effort has been made to fulfil requirements with regard to reproducing
copyright material. The author and publisher will be glad to rectify any
omissions at the earliest opportunity.

www.orionbooks.co.uk

'True Love
Never Dies'